GERMAN MILITARY TRAILERS AND TOWED EQUIPMENT

A flatbed trailer for transporting armored vehicles (Sd.Ah. 115) serving with the Afrikakorps. On the trailer is a Panzerjäger I, a 47mm Czech anti-tank gun mounted on the chassis of the Panzer I B.

1935-1945

Horst Beiersdorf

Schiffer Military/Aviation History
Atglen, PA

Acknowledgements

My special thanks go to my sons Holger and Ulrich as well as to the library of Military District II, Hannover, without whose support this illustrated volume would not have been possible.

Photographs and information were made available by Reinhard Frank, Horst Scheibert, Kurt Schulz-Eisenhardt, Walter Spielberger. Karl R. Pawlas, the Rheinmetall Firm and others.

Sources: Wehrmacht service manuals (H.Dv., L.Dv., D.), Waffen Arsenal (WA) and Waffen-Revue (WR).

Preface

This book brings to the reader a collection of photos of Wehrmacht equipment never before included in a single work. We ask that the reader excuse the quality of the photo reproduction. This is due to grainy photos and the yellowed paper of old Wehrmacht service manuals. The few photos that were taken (and in most cases the trailer was not the actual subject) do not provide a large selection from which to choose. Furthermore we ask the reader to forgive the use once again of photographs published in earlier volumes. Today the trailers in the background are subjects of interest, just as the illustrated weapons and vehicles were at the time the photos were taken.

Holzlager

Führungsstück

Zugöse

The steel field trailer was introduced by the Wehrmacht as Army Vehicle 7 (Hf.7). From 1936 on, it served with infantry rifle companies and platoons as a large combat trailer (Hf.7/11) and was used to carry the soldiers' equipment, including packs. It was also equipped with a towing fork, so that it could be pulled by a truck or Raupenschlepper Ost (RSO) if necessary. (H.Dv.476/1)

Translated from the German by David Johnston

Printed in the United States of America.
ISBN: 0-88740-757-9

This title was originally published under the title,
Waffen-Arsenal Waffen und Fahrzeuge der Heere und Luftstreitkräfte KFZ-Anhänger der Wehrmacht 1935-1945,
by Podzun-Pallas-Verlag, Friedberg.

Published by Schiffer Publishing Ltd.
77 Lower Valley Road
Atglen, PA 19310
Please write for a free catalog.
This book may be purchased from the publisher.
Please include $2.95 postage.
Try your bookstore first.

We are interested in hearing from authors
with book ideas on related topics.

Motor Vehicle Trailers of the Wehrmacht

After the publication of more than 140 photo albums by Waffen-Arsenal, I thought it appropriate to produce an illustrated volume dealing with the Wehrmacht's motor vehicle trailers as well. One can say without exaggeration that the Wehrmacht would have had no motorized units if there had been no trailers.

After a systematic examination of several hundred books and photo albums as well as service manuals, I have amassed text and photo information on the subject without, however, making any claim to completeness. I have also discovered that photos were not available of every trailer. I hope that more information and photos will come my way the appearance of this photo album.

For simplicity's sake I have divided the trailers into four groups: special trailers with special trailer numbers, and trailers without numbers, grouped single-, twin- and multi-axle.

Special Trailers with Numbers

Special Trailer Designation

1	Trailer (single-axle) for kleines Kettenkrad
1/1	Trailer (single-axle) for kleines Kettenkrad
1/2	Trailer (single-axle) for kleines Kettenkrad for heavy field wire
3	Trailer (single-axle) for light loads
4	Trailer (single-axle) for medium and heavy loads
5	Trailer (single-axle) for artillery ammunition
7	Trailer(single-axle) for Nebelwerfer ammunition

Special Trailer Designation

8	Trailer (single-axle) for veterinary equiment
11	Trailer (single-axle) for disinfecting with shower installation
13	Trailer (single-axle) for 100 H.P. MB motor-boat
41	
15	Trailer (single-axle) for ferry cable
20	Trailer (single-axle) for underground cable
21	Trailer (twin-axle) for telephone construction units

Sonder Anhänger Ost 1½ t

This trailer's complete designation was Trailer (Multi-axle) 1 1/2 ton for RSO (Raupenschlepper Ost). It was manufactured by various firms and was designed to be used with the Raupenschlepper Ost or any other similarly slow vehicle. Payload was 1,500 kilograms and maximum permissible weight was 2,170 kilograms. The 1000x180mm wheels were disc wheels with iron road surfaces.

Right and below right: The artillery trailer (single-axle) for light loads (Sd.Ah.3) was used to transport the 75mm leF.K.16 light field cannon and the 105mm leFH 16 light field howitzer. Payload was 1,470 kg. Both guns lacked springs and had wooden-spoked wheels with iron tires and were thus unsuitable for towing by motor vehicle. Loading them on this trailer allowed the guns to be transported by the medium prime mover (Sd.Kfz.7). (H.Dv.446/2)

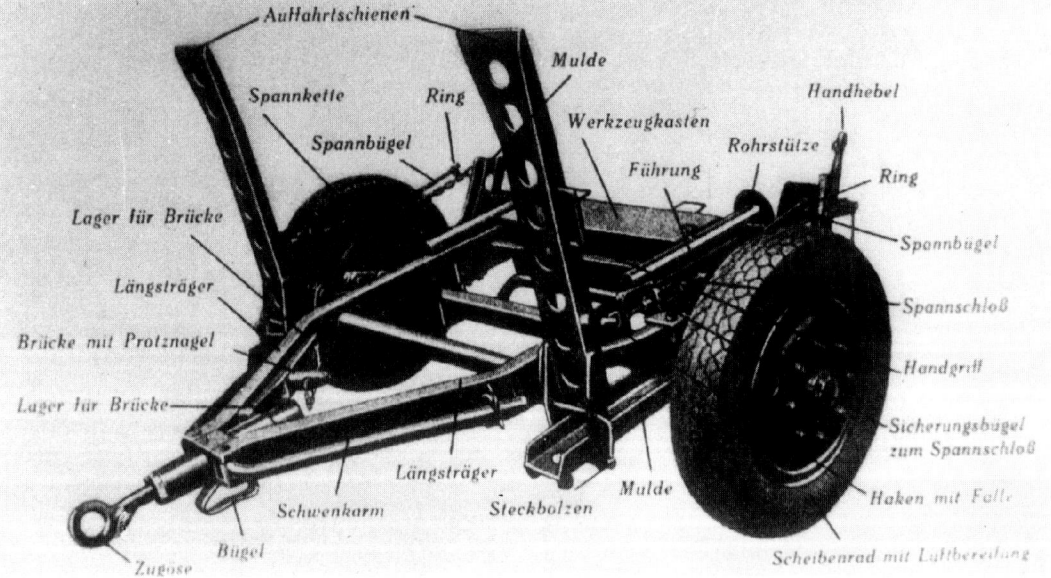

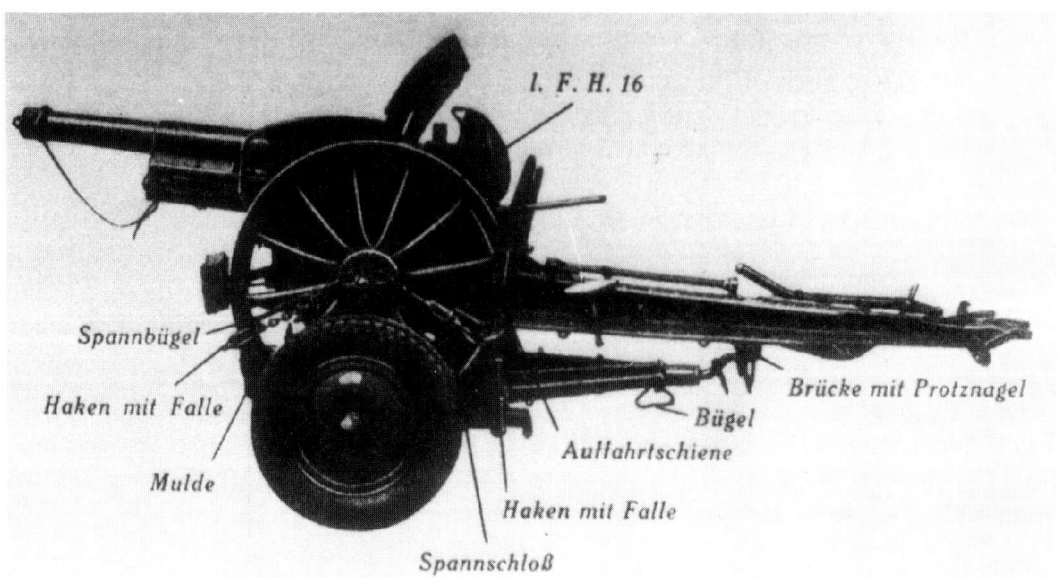

The artillery trailer (single-axle) for medium and heavy loads (Sd.Ah.4) weighed 1,500 kilograms and had a payload of 3,300 kg. This allowed the 150mm Heavy Field Howitzer 13, which weighed 2,250 kg., to be towed by motor vehicle. (D 600)

Disinfecting trailer with shower device (Sd.Ah.11). These were assigned to medical squads and were used to disinfect (delouse) uniforms, which were could be simultaneously washed under the shower installation. (H.Dv. 195/5)

The trailer (single-axle) for motorboat (Sd.Ah.13) was used by combat engineer units to transport the 100 H.P. M-Boot 28 or the 100 H.P. M-Boot 41 and was included as part of the pioneer bridge column. Payload was 2,200 kg. and the trailer itself weighed 2,000 kg. The trailer was normally pulled by the 3-ton medium truck (6x4) or the 5-ton medium prime mover (Sd.Kfz.6). (D 600)

Below: The trailer (single-axle) for ferry cable (Sd.Ah.15) was included as part of the pioneer bridge column's reserve platoon and was towed by the 3-ton medium truck (6x4). It was used to guide the pioneer ferries from shore to shore on cable. (H.Dv. 220/3a)

The Sd.Ah.20 (single-axle) trailer was used by signals units to lay underground cable. The contents of the trailer were a drum with 500 meters of underground cable, pickaxes, spades and shovels. (D 600)

Below: The Sd.Ah.21 (twin-axle) trailer was used by the signals corps and consisted of two single-axle trailers linked together. The trailer was used to transport telephone poles for construction of above-ground telephone lines. Weighing 800 kilograms, the Sd.Ah.21 had a payload of 3,700 kg. (D 600)

The Sd.Ah.23 single-axle trailer was also designed for the signals corps and carried a Type D Battery Charger. It was towed by the Kfz.42 battery truck in light signals columns and was used to charge the spare batteries carried in the battery truck. (D 906 + 930)

Below: This photo shows the Sd.Ah.23 and the battery truck during charging of the batteries. Adequate ventilation was an absolute necessity during the charging procedure, as the acid mist and steam produced by the charging process were explosive in poorly-ventilated areas. (D 906)

Based on the Sd.Ah.23, the generator trailer (single-axle) with 220/65 V, 4.5/1.3 kW generator, was used by the forward artillery. (D 298/17)

The Sd.Ah.24 was a single-axle trailer on which was mounted an A-Type Heavy Generator (220/380 Volts, 12 Kilowatts, 25 Amperes) for use by the signal corps' heavy motorized radio units (a, b and c). The trailer was towed by the Kfz.72 heavy radio truck. The trailer was also used by maintenance units to power machinery, in which case it was towed by the Kfz.79 maintenance truck. (D 621/3)

The Sd.Ah.25 was the first, open version of a single-axle trailer for field trunk wire. It was used to transport 4 drums of field trunk wire, 1 reel cart and equipment for the rapid laying of short lines or for troubleshooting. The trailer was towed by an Kfz.15. (D 731/5)

Below: Version II of the Sd.Ah.25 with enclosed superstructure. On the front of the trailer are racks for the wheels of the Field Trunk Wire Cable-laying Vehicle. Both trailers used the Luftwaffe A 1 Standard Chassis.

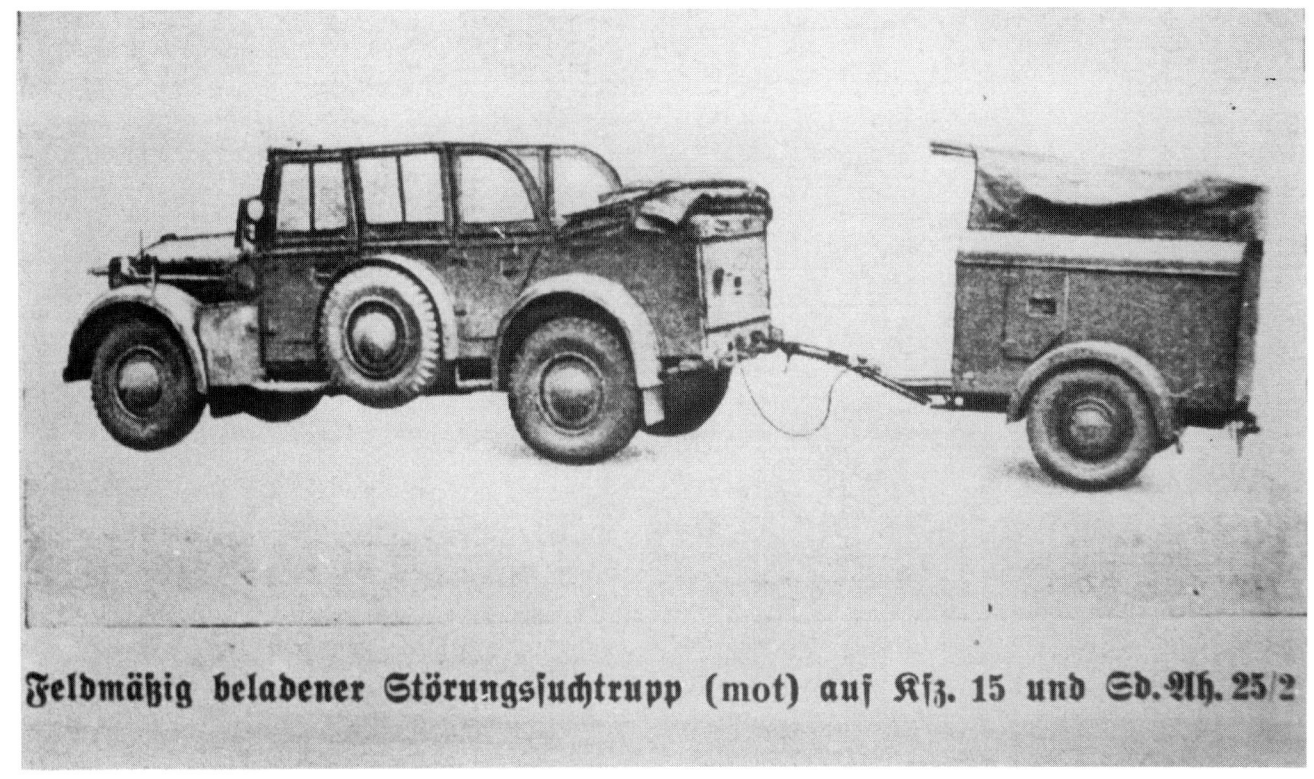

Feldmäßig beladener Störungssuchtrupp (mot) auf Kfz. 15 und Sd.Ah. 25/2

The Sd.Ah.25/2 was a single-axle trailer with signals equipment for troubleshooting teams. Stowed on top of the trailer were a soil tamper, long spade, shovel and folding ladder. Inside the trailer were two drums, each with 250 meters of trunk wire, 16 porcelain double-bell insulators, 1 safety belt and 1 pair of crampons, as well as tools and small parts. (D 719)

Below: The Sd.Ah.32 was used to transport ammunition for the 37mm anti-tank gun. Payload was 390 kg. with a maximum allowable weight of 780 kg. The Kfz.12, Kfz.69 or light 1-ton prime mover (Sd.Kfz.10) were used to tow the trailer. (D 600)

The Sd.Ah.33 single-axle trailer was used to transport Nebelwerfer (multiple rocket launcher) ammunition. Payload was 360 kg. with a maximum allowable load of 700 kg. (D 600)

Below: The Sd.Ah.35 was a dough-mixing trailer for use by motorized bakery companies and was towed by a truck. It was used to make bread dough and took about 5-8 minutes to mix 145-150 kilograms of ingredients. It was possible to prepare approximately 1,100 to 1,800 kilograms of dough in an hour. (H.Dv.498/3)

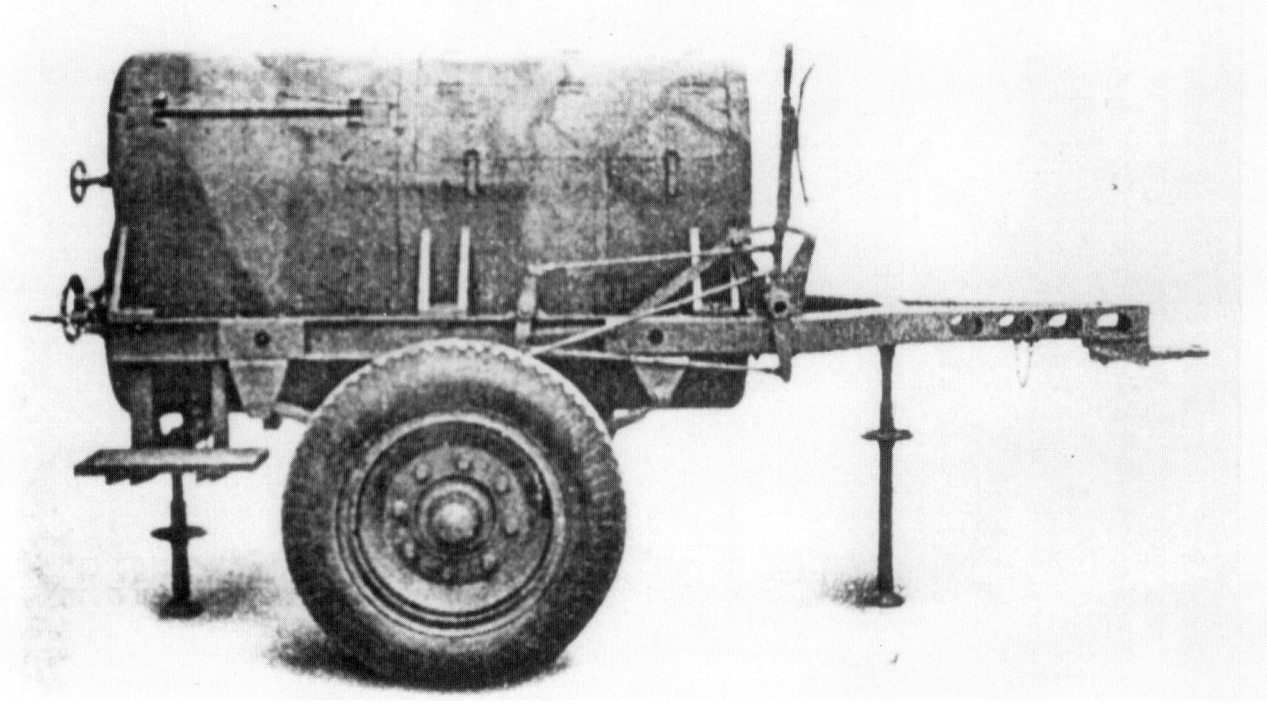

Teigknetanhänger (umgeändert)
(Sd. Ah. 35)

This Sd.Ah.35 trailer looks the same as the one in the previous illustration, but is in fact a converted horse-drawn administrative vehicle (Vwf.2). All-up weight was 1,100 kg. (H.Dv.489/3)

Below: The Sd.Ah.51 single-axle trailer was designed to transport the 20mm Flak 30 and Flak 38 anti-aircraft guns as well as the ammunition boxes for the 20mm guns. Standard tractor was the Light Flak Vehicle (Kfz.81). (H.Dv. 177 + L.Dv. 610)

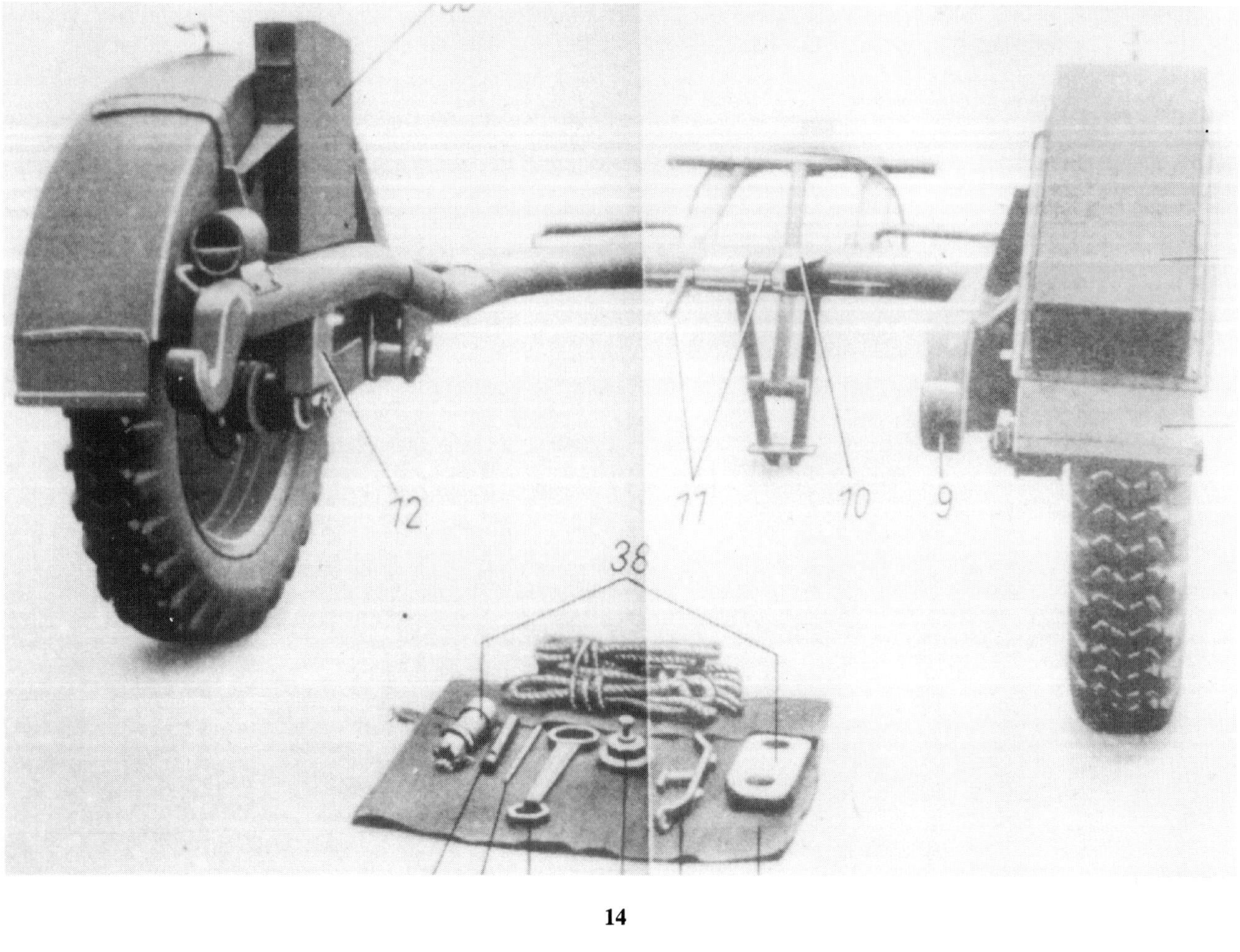
12
11
10
9
38

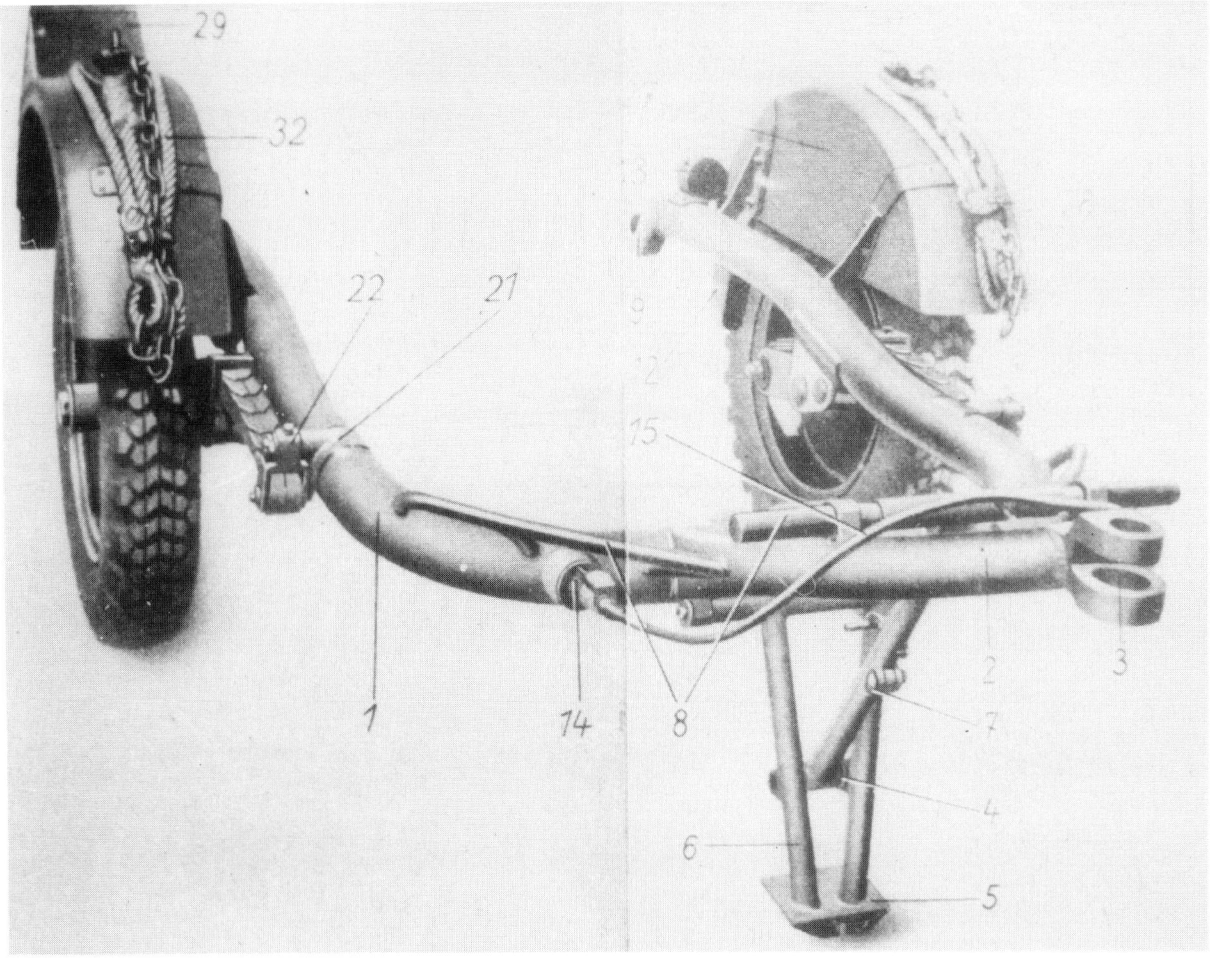

Sd.Ah.51. With only minor modifications the 20mm Flak trailer could be used to transport the 600mm anti-aircraft searchlight. It was towed by a Kraftwagen I or II (Kfz.83). Weight of the trailer was 342 kg. (L.Dv.610)

Right:
Sd.Ah.53 single-axle trailer for transport of the Kommandohilfsgerät 35 auxiliary fire director. The trailer weighed 605 kg. and its payload was 565 kilograms. Standard tow vehicle was the Anti-aircraft Range-finder Squad Vehicle (Kfz.74). (D 600)

Left:
Sd.Ah.52 trailer (single-axle) for transporting the 20mm four-barrelled flak, the 37mm Flak 36, the Data Computer 40 and the accessory and ammunition boxes for the four-barrelled flak or 37mm Flak 36. Trailer weight was 870 kg. with a payload of 1,700 kg. (D 600)

Left:
Sd.Ah.54. This single-axle trailer weighed 800 kilograms and had a payload of 450 kg. Nothing has been learned as to its purpose, but as it has a number in the fifties it must have been used for some type of flak equipment.

Right:
Sd.Ah.55. Trailer for anti-aircraft range-finder. Trailer weight 1,150 kg. Payload 650 kg. (D 600)

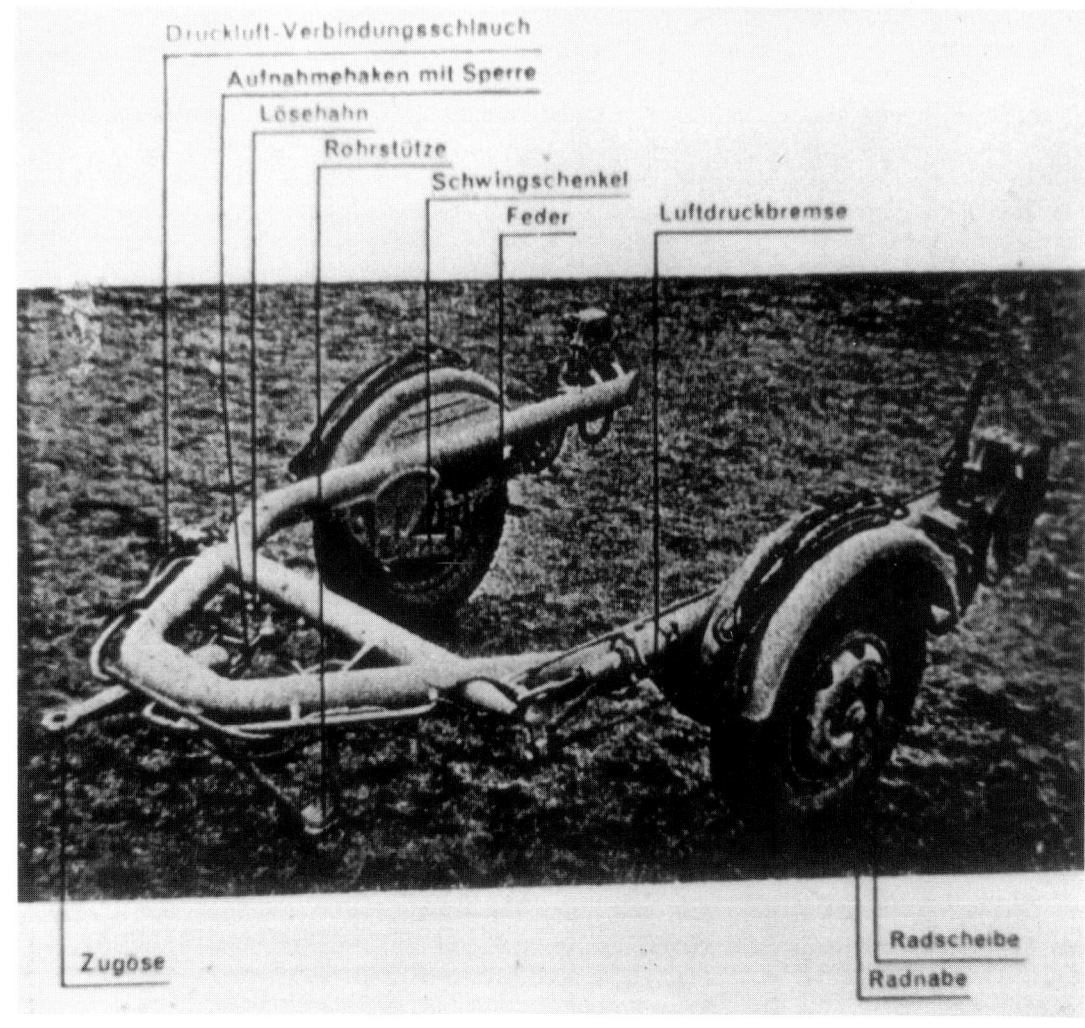

Druckluft-Verbindungsschlauch
Aufnahmehaken mit Sperre
Lösehahn
Rohrstütze
Schwingschenkel
Feder
Luftdruckbremse
Zugöse
Radscheibe
Radnabe

Sd.Ah.58 single-axle trailer for transporting the 37mm Flak 43. Empty weight 650 kg. (L.Dv.T 1054/1)

Left:
Sd.Ah.103 twin-axle trailer for medium and heavy loads. The trailer weighed 1,200 kg. and its payload was 3,200 kg. Used for motor transport of the 105mm leFH 16 light field howitzer. Tow vehicle was the 8-ton prime mover (Sd.Kfz.7). (D 600)

Right:
With a payload of 2,500 kg., the Sd.Ah.104 twin-axle trailer was used to transport the 37mm Flak 18, Type 36 Data Computer, trumpet-type sound locator, 1500mm searchlight, 24 kW medium generator and SSW machinery vehicle. The trailer weighed 1,830 kg. Tractor was the medium 3-ton truck (6x4). (D 600)

Sd.Ah.105 bakery trailer. The trailer was an unmodified bakery oven trailer (Vwf.1 = Administrative Vehicle 1), which saw service with bakery companies in the First World War, on pneumatic tires. 80 loaves of bread could be baked in approximately two hours. (H.Dv.489/2)

Sd.Ah.106.
More modern version of the bakery trailer. It was used to make bread for the field army when it could not be supplied by fixed bakeries. As a rule bakery companies were equipped with 5 bakery trailers. One oven could bake 160 loaves of bread in two hours, and a bakery company could therefore deliver approximately 9,600 loaves in 24 hours, using 8,000 to 9,000 liters of water and about 180 kg. of brown coal or wood. (H.Dv.489/1)

Sd.Ah.107.
Single-axle trailer with large-capacity refrigerator unit. (D 600)

Sd.Ah.108
Twin-axle trailer for transporting 3 Type 39 Pioneer Assault Boats with motors and accessories. Either the 3-ton medium truck (6x4) or the 5-ton medium prime mover (Sd.Kfz.6) was used as tractor. Trailer weight (without boats) was 1,450 kilograms and payload 1,550 kg. (D 600)

Sd.Ah.111
Twin-axle trailer used as a heavy survey trailer by surveying and mapping units with a payload of 4,400 kg. (D 600)

Sd.Ah.115
Flatbed trailer for tanks with a payload of 10 tons. Light Divisions used the trailer to transport the Panzer I and II, in which case it was towed by a Faun or Büssing 9-ton truck. Tank recovery platoons used the trailer to transport damaged tanks, using an 8-ton prime mover to pull the trailer. The trailer's rear axle was removed for loading. Overall length was 9.68 meters and loaded weight was 15,000 kilograms. (D 600)

The Sd.Ah.116 flatbed trailer was built for a payload of 22 tons; it was used to transport tanks and other loads within its payload range and dimensions. It consisted of a front chassis, the loading bridge and the rear chassis. The forward chassis and the loading bridge combined to make a loading ramp. The rear chassis had an Ackerman steering mechanism which was independent of the front chassis; it was controlled by a steering arm from the steering wheel. The driver of the trailer had to demonstrate driving ability equivalent to that of a holder of a Class 2 driver's license. The trailer's overall length was 14.4 meters. (D 617/3)

Sd.Ah.21
With a payload of 60 tons, this flatbed trailer was used to transport heavy tanks of the Tiger class. It was part of the equipment of maintenance companies of Tiger and Panther battalions. Firm, dry roads were necessary if the trailer was to be used for the recovery of damaged tanks. Standard tractor was the 18-ton heavy prime mover (Sd.Kfz.9). (W. Spielberger)

Abb. 11
Sonderanhänger 201 mit eingesetztem Verbindungsstück

Sd.Ah.201.
Twin-axle trailer for transporting the 88mm Flak 18 and the 88mm anti-tank gun derived from it. Tractor was the 8-ton medium prime mover (Sd.Kfz.7) or the 12-ton heavy prime mover (Sd.Kfz.8).

Sd.Ah.202
This trailer was used to transport the 88mm Flak 36, 37 and 41 anti-aircraft guns. It consisted of two identical single-axle trailers, either of which could be used as the front or rear element. Tractor for the trailer and gun was the 12-ton heavy prime mover (Sd.Kfz.8). Weight of the trailer was 3,200 kg., payload 6,000 kg. (D 600)

Sd.Ah.203
This trailer was used to transport the 105mm Flak 39 and the gun carriage of the 128mm Flak 40/2 with driving frame. The two twin-axle trailers were identical and either could be used as the front or rear element of the combination. Tractor was the 12-ton heavy prime mover (Sd.Kfz.8). Trailer weight 4,500 kg., payload 10,000 kg. (D 600)

Sd.Ah.204.
Two-part trailer for transporting the following equipment:
50mm Flak 41, 120 V 60kW generator, 2000mm searchlight, barrage balloon winch, FuMG 41 T "Mannheim" revolving platform (navy). Trailer weight 2,375 kg., payload 4,500 kg., overall length 6.50 meters. (D 600)

Right:
Sd.Ah.206
This trailer was used to transport the 37mm Flakzwilling 43 double-barrel anti-aircraft gun, 55mm Flakgerät 58 "Schmetterling" (Butterfly) anti-aircraft rocket, 2000mm Type 43 searchlight, 120 kW generator. It could also be used as a replacement for the Sd.Ah.104 without modification. The two identical single-axle chassis were interchangeable. Standard tractor was the 4.5-ton truck. (L.Dv.T 1054/1)

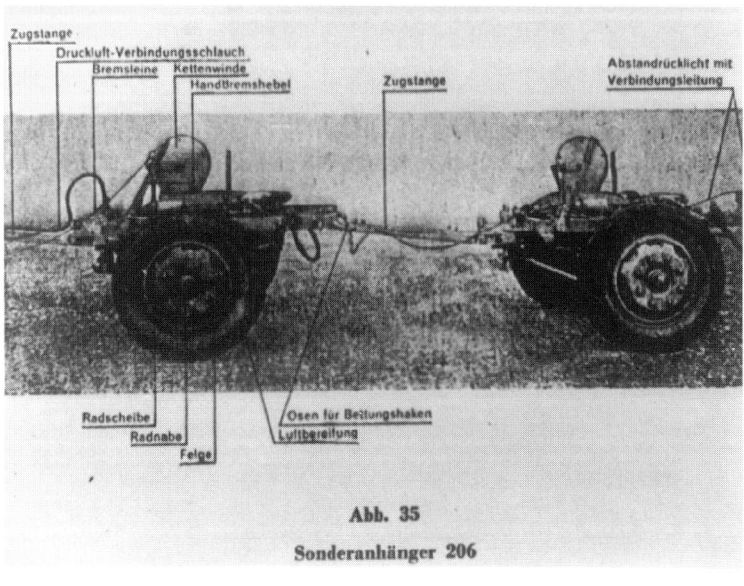

Abb. 35
Sonderanhänger 206

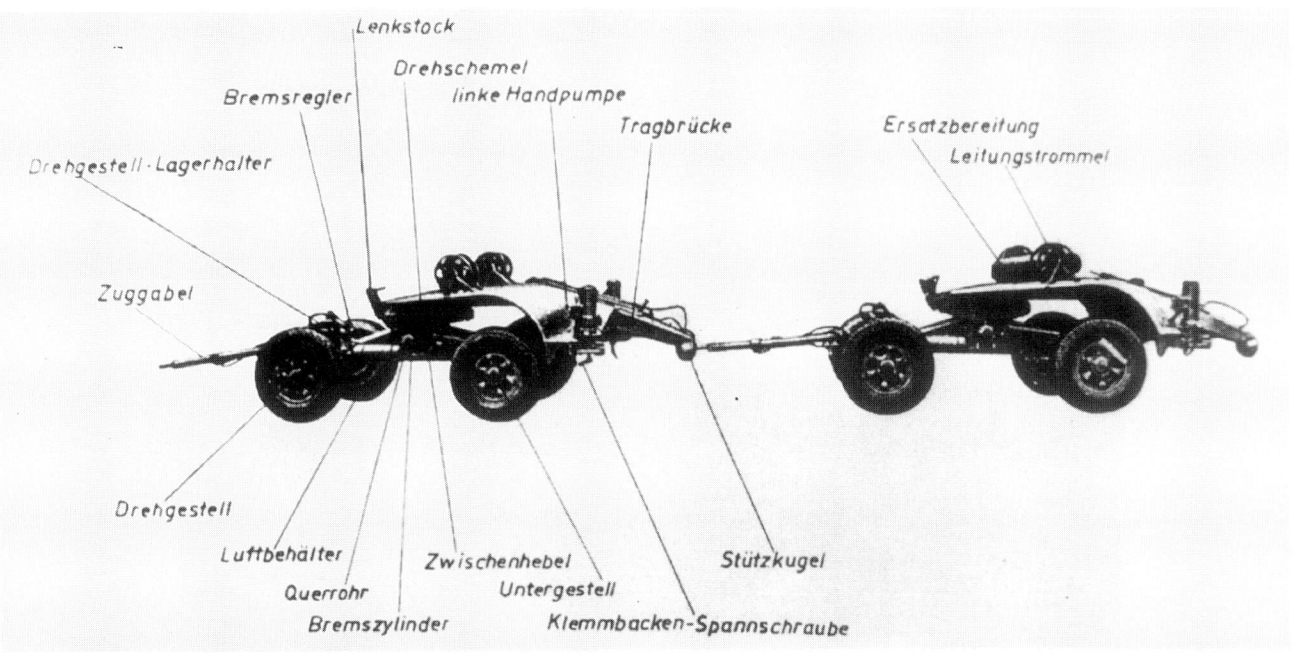

Labels (clockwise/around diagram):
Lenkstock
Drehschemel
Bremsregler
linke Handpumpe
Tragbrücke
Ersatzbereitung
Leitungstrommel
Drehgestell·Lagerhalter
Zuggabel
Drehgestell
Luftbehälter
Zwischenhebel
Stützkugel
Querrohr
Untergestell
Bremszylinder
Klemmbacken-Spannschraube

Sd.Ah.220
Four-axle trailer for transporting the 128mm Flak 40/1 in one piece with the 18-ton heavy prime mover (Sd.Kfz.9). Weight of the special trailer and gun was 27,000 kg.

Ah.301
Single-axle trailer used by the Luftwaffe as a tank sprayer (Kfz.343). The trailer contained hoses and equipment to make the pumper, which was an air-field fire-fighting vehicle, into a vehicle suitable for all types of fire-fighting missions. Trailer weight 670 kg., payload 580 kg. (D 600)

Ah.302
Single-axle trailer for the Luftwaffe's hose tender (Kfz.344). The trailer was equipped with a suction pump, hoses and equipment, allowing the hose tender to be used as a fire-fighting vehicle. Trailer weight 650 kg., payload 710 kg. (D 600)

Left:
Ah.422
Navigation radio direction-finder trailer (single-axle). Trailer weight 1,375 kg., payload 750 kg. (D 600)

The single-axle field kitchen trailer (Sd.Ah.401) was standard Luftwaffe equipment and was allocated to units with personnel strengths of up to 170 men. The kitchen produced hot food and drinks. Food could be boiled, fried or steamed. While on the march the field kitchen could only be used to make one-pot meals. One field-kitchen soldier was sufficient to operate the kitchen. The cooking pot had a usable capacity of 200 L, however for cooking it was designed to take just 175 liters and could also be used as an automatic cooker. The coffee cauldron had a usable capacity of 90 liters and the frying pan about 35 liters. Driving speed of the pneumatic-tired field kitchen was up to 110 kph. The steel-wheeled field kitchen was transported on another vehicle.

Ah.447
Luftwaffe navigation radio direction-finder trailer (twin-axle). Maximum allowable weight 4,250 kg. (D 600)

Below: Sd.Ah.450
Six-meter trailer for transporting aircraft wings. Trailer wight 1,700 kg., payload 500 kg. (D 600)

Sd.Ah.451
Ten-meter trailer for transporting aircraft wings. Trailer weight 2,400 kg., payload 1,000 kg. (D 600)

Ah.454
Trailer version of aviation fuel tank truck. Trailer weight 4,200 kg., payload 2,625 kg. (D 600)

Ah.468
Luftwaffe telephone switchboard trailer (twin-axle). Trailer weight 3,360 kg., loaded weight 5.480 kg., overall length 6,800 mm. (D 600)

Ah.469
Luftwaffe teletype coupling trailer (twin-axle). Trailer weight 2,520 kg., loaded weight 3,350 kg., overall length 6,800 mm. (D 600)

Ah.470
Luftwaffe radio trailer (short wave/long wave). Trailer weight 3,200 kg., loaded weight 3,600 kg., overall length 5,480 mm. (D 600)

Ah.471
Luftwaffe radio-receiver operations trailer. Trailer weight 3,100 kg., loaded weight 3,600 kg., overall length 5,600 mm. (D 600)

Ah.472
Light Luftwaffe beacon light trailer (twin-axle). Trailer weight 3,115 kg., loaded weight 4,500 kg., overall length 5,540 mm.
(D 600)

Ah.473
Medium Luftwaffe beacon light trailer (twin-axle). Trailer weight 3,115 kg., loaded weight 4,500 kg., overall length 5,540 mm. (D 600)

Ah.51
Illumination trailer (twin-axle) with a 1,300 cc 17 H.P. gasoline motor powering a 220 V 6 kW electric motor. Trailer weight 2,680 kg., loaded weight 4,680 kg., overall length 5,500 mm. (D 600)

Sd.Ah.32/3
Single-axle trailer for the schwere Panzerbüchse 41 heavy anti-tank rifle on light field carriage. Trailer weight 85 kg., loaded weight 260 kg. Driving speed 80 kph. (W.R. Nr.58)

Single-Axle Trailers without Special Trailer (Sd.Ah.) Numbers

Trailer chassis (single-axle) 900 kg.
Trailer chassis (single-axle) 1,500 kg., Type 41
Trailer chassis (single-axle) 1,900 kg.
Trailer chassis (single-axle) 500 kg.
Trailer chassis (single-axle) 900 kg.
Trailer chassis (single-axle) 1,500 kg.
Trailer chassis (single-axle) 2,200 kg.
A 1 open 0.5-ton trailer, Luftwaffe
A-1 open 0.5-ton trailer as hose reel trailer for the Kfz.346 fire truck
Open trailer with enclosed superstructure used by railway engineers and vehicle parks
Trailer for standard fuel container
Trailer for 200-liter fuel drum
Trailer for 2 x 200-liter fuel drums
Trailer for heavy spigot mortar
Trailer for pioneer inflatable motorboat (commercially-available equipment)
Trailer with 12 kVA emergency generator, "Carfaris" diesel engine, navy
Trailer with 12 kVA emergency generator, "Fimag" gasoline engine, navy
Trailer for the schwere Panzerbüchse 41 anti-tank rifle
Trailer for mange gas tanks
Trailer for classified documents of survey and mapping units
Open trailer for equipment of veterinary (horse) hospitals
Trailer with V 2 launch platform
Burnout antenna trailer for operational long-range rocket units
Type-C BS trailer
Large air compressor as trailer
Paratrooper cart as trailer for the Kettenkrad
Large field kitchen as trailer
Fortress cable-jointing cart
Fortress cable-measuring cart
Heavy plough (decontamination) as trailer
Hand cart for light spigot mortar, combat engineers
Small wire drum trailer for long-range rocket units
Guide-beam antenna trailer for long-range rocket units
Guide-beam control trailer for long-range rocket units
Arc welder generator on 1,500kg trailer
110/220 V 24 kW generator, mobile unit in trailer
220 V (A/C) 15/18 kVA, medical units
220 V 6.5 kW generator, mobile unit in trailer
220/380 V (rotary current) 30 kVA, mobile unit in trailer
Motor pump, mobile unit in open trailer
Light spray trailer
Suction pump trailer (Tgsa 8) (1937 model)
Suction pump trailer (Tgsa 8) (1939 model)
Suction pump trailer (open)
Trough trailer for decontamination vehicle (Kfz.305/122) of the S.H.D.
T-Stoff (concentrated hydrogen peroxide) pre-heater for long-range rocket units
1,000-liter water trailer

Type 41 1,500 kg trailer chassis (single-axle). The chassis was developed from components of the multi-axle vehicle trailer and was fitted with various bodies. Various firms were involved in production of the chassis and all parts were interchangeable. (D 691/41)

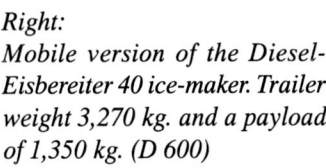

Right:
Mobile version of the Diesel-Eisbereiter 40 ice-maker. Trailer weight 3,270 kg. and a payload of 1,350 kg. (D 600)

Left:
Large Druckerlufterzeuger 34 air compressor installed in a trailer. (D 600)

The Fortress Cable Jointing Cart was equipped with soldering and switching equipment and tools and was part of the signals equipment set of cable switching squads. It was used to extend and maintain the wire networks and switching points of land fortifications. Cable switching squads were equipped with six cable-jointing carts. As a motor vehicle trailer a speed of up to 40 kph was allowed on firm roads, 20 kph on secondary roads and level terrain. The cart was loaded on to a truck for longer journeys. (D 797/1)

The Fortress Cable Measuring Cart also belonged to the signals equipment set of cable switching squads. It contained all the measuring instruments and equipment necessary for measuring, cable finding, elimination of faults and so on. When pulled by a motor vehicle the same restrictions applied as those of the Fortress Cable Jointing Cart. (D 797/2)

Left:
The Paratrooper Cart was pulled by a Kettenkrad (Sd.Kfz.2). Here it is being used as an ammunition vehicle for the Leichtgeschütz 2 100mm light gun.

Below:
Decontamination plow as used by the chemical warfare units. It was intended that these would plow 1-1.2-meter-deep furrows through contaminated terrain, allowing the infantry to pass through without being affected. The device was never used in its intended role, however about 200 such plows saw action on the Eastern Front from September 1943 as trench-diggers, pulled by a 3-ton light prime mover. The plow was operated by the driver of the prime mover by means of a pressure-oil (hydraulic) line.

Left:
In order to increase the radius of action of the panzers a version of the fuel trailer was also developed to transport two fuel drums. According to former Leutnant Spielberger, the army had more than 1,860 of these trailers for the Panzer IV and its derivatives. (Photo: Spielberger)

Trailer for the transport of the Heavy Spigot Mortar in three loads. The photo shows Trailer 1 loaded with parts of the mortar. (Waffen-Revue 15)

Ammunition trailer for the Heavy Spigot Mortar. (Waffen-Revue 15)

Trailer with arc-welder field generator, which was removable from the 1,500 kg. standard trailer chassis. Used by tank maintenance platoons. (D 622/9)

Generating unit (Benzol) 110/220 V, equal to approximately 24 kW. Mobile generator for powering machinery and power tools used in wood and metal work by the combat engineers. Output of the Magirus internal-combustion engine was 48-50 H.P., that of the electrical generator (Siemens-Schuckert Direct Current Generator) 24 kW. The unit's fuel consumption was 15 liters per hour. (H.Dv.288/1)

Right:
Motor pump installed in trailer as a mobile unit. 585cc motor, 14.5 H.P. Pump line 400-600 liters per minute. Rate of fuel consumption 6-7 liters per hour. (D 600)

Above: Special trailer for the Panzerbüchse 41, with two loading ramps for the anti-tank rifle and a container for ammunition boxes. (W-R.58)

Suction Pump Trailer 8 (Tgsa 8) 1937 model. The trailer's load included an 800 liter per minute suction pump, 6 A-Type suction hoses, 5 B-Type pressure hoses, rigid pipe, elevated hydrant key and 2 portable hose drums. Tractor was the KzS 8 fire truck based on the 1937 model Opel Blitz 1-ton truck. (L.Dv.783/2a)

Left:
Suction Pump Trailer 8 (Tgsa 8) 1939 model. Equipment load was similar to that of the 1937 model. The trailer was pulled by the 1.5-ton fire truck (Lskw) based on the 1939 model Opel Blitz. (L.Dv.783/2b)

Right:
Suction pump trailer (open). Motor 909cc, 18 H.P. Pumping efficiency 800 liters per minute. The trailer was pulled by the Opel Blitz 1.5-ton fire-fighting vehicle, 1939 model. (D 600)

Below:
Trough trailer for the Kfz.305/122 decontamination vehicle based on the 1941 Opel Blitz Type 3.6-36 S of the Safety and Emergency Service (S.H.D). (L.Dv.783/5)

Twin-Axle Trailers without Special Trailer Numbers

A 2 standard 1-ton open trailer
A 2 trailer with generator, navy
A 2 trailer as hose reel trailer for the Kfz.346 fire truck, 1936 and 1941 models
B 2 standard 3-ton open trailer
B 2 C trailer with 220/380 V rotating current 60 kVA generator for the armored forces, combat engineers and Luftwaffe
B 3 standard 4.5-ton open trailer, Luftwaffe
E 5 standard 5-ton trailer
E 8 standard 8-ton trailer
Trailer with equipment for filling the oxygen systems of combat aircraft
Trailer (long wooden type) for six loading ramps, part of the pioneer bridge equipment for constructing the light Z-Bridge
Trailer with medium fuel tank installation (open), Luftwaffe
Trailer with heavy fuel tank installation (open), Luftwaffe
Trailer with Feldballonwinde 40 field balloon winch, artillery
Trailer with Hazemeyer anti-aircraft data computer, navy
Trailer with 20mm Flak 30 on pedestal mount
Trailer with tank containing liquid oxygen for long-range rockets
Trailer with 30-centimeter crank-type telescopic mast, signals units
1.5-ton trailer for the Raupenschlepper Ost caterpillar tractor
Trailer for 200 H.P. tow boat used by the combat engineers
Amphibious trailer for the Land-Water Tractor built by Kässbohrer
Decontamination trailer for the decontamination equipment vehicle (Kfz.305/123)
Cable drum trailer for long-range rocket units
Vehicle maintenance trailer for long-range rocket units
Runway illumination trailer, Luftwaffe
Air compressor trailer for long-range rocket units
Omnibus trailer, Kässbohrer Type P 4 1939
Rohrwagen 40 barrel trailer for the 128mm Flak 40
Frame saw on trailer, combat engineers
Searchlight transport trailer with old-style G 150 searchlight, naval artillery
Searchlight transport trailer with G 110 searchlight, naval artillery
16-ton Strabo crane as trailer
Aircraft wing transport trailer a and b (1939 model), Luftwaffe
V 2 transport trailer, Vidal Factory
Hydrogen compressor trailer 41 + 42, artillery
Hydrogen developer trailer 40 + 41, artillery

Multi-Axle Trailers without Special Trailer Numbers

8-ton, three-axle trailer for the 600 H.P. Type 43 motorboat, used by amphibious landing pioneers
Three-axle open trailer with a payload of 11,000 kg.
Three-axle trailer with 30-ton crane
Three-axle amphibious trailer with 10-ton payload
Three-axle amphibious trailer with 20-ton payload
Three-axle trailer for the A 4 (V 2) long-range rocket, Meiller Factory
Four-axle trailer for heavy loads, Culemeyer Factory
Six-axle trailer for heavy loads up to 60 tons, Culemeyer Factory
Six-axle trailer for heavy loads up to 60 tons, Gotha Rail Car Factory
Trailer for heavy loads up to 110 tons
Trailer for heavy loads up to 150 tons

Left:
Trailer with firing platform for the A-4 (V-2) long-range rocket. The trailer was assigned Position Number 103 in the long-range rocket ground installation. The trailer was pulled by an 8-ton KM m 11 medium prime mover (Sd.Kfz.7) on which was mounted an armored fire-control vehicle. The combination was assigned Position Number 101. (W. Spielberger)

Right:
0.75-ton A 2 Standard Trailer as hose reel trailer for the 1936 and 1941 model hose trucks (Kfz.346). The trailer's load consisted of 8 B-Type pressure hoses on wheeled reels, 22 C-Type pressure hoses on wheeled reels, 1 bicycle, 1 inflatable boat, 1 swivelling nozzle holder. (L.Dv.783/3 + 783/3a)

Bild 5: Anh mit Planverdeck, linke Seite

1 Planverdeck

Left:
5-ton E 5 Standard Trailer built by various manufacturers. The chassis was fitted with a 600-mm-high wooden-board-bed body on the production line. Special bodies could be installed. Loaded weight 7,600 kg. Payload 5,000 kg. Wheel track front and rear 1,735 mm. Wheelbase 2940 mm. (D 692/41)

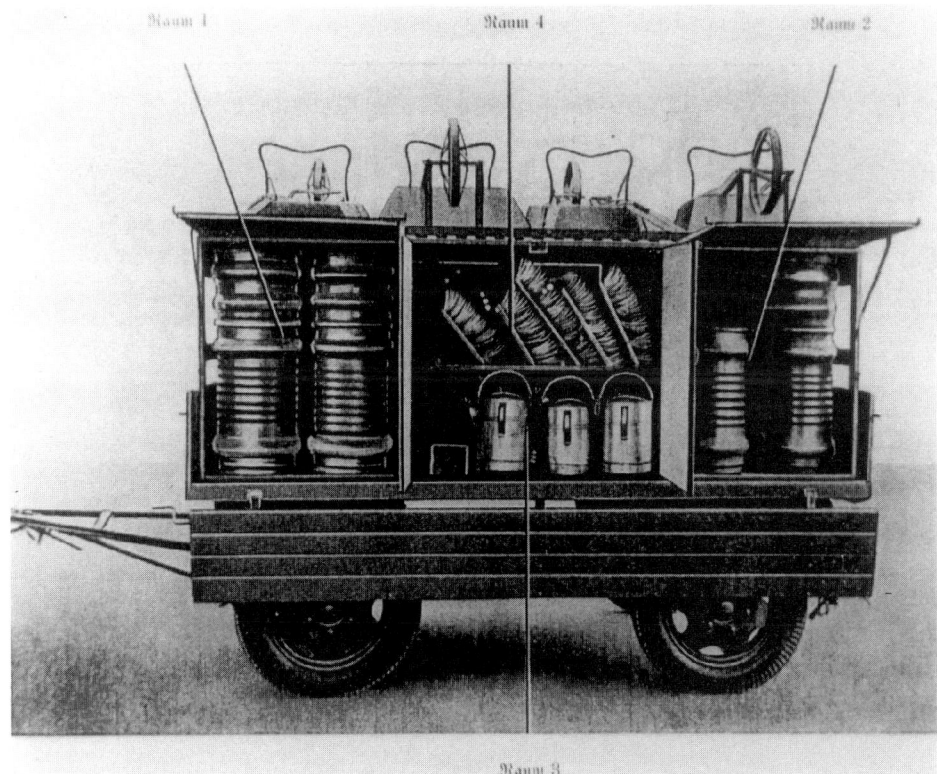

Top photo:
Decontamination trailer for the 1941-model decontamination equipment truck (Kfz.305/123) as used by the Safety and Emergency Service (S.H.D.)

The photo at the bottom of the page offers a good view of the contents of the trailer. These included 10 50-kg drums and 20 25-kg drums of decontamination agent, 1 50-kg drum of gas-detection powder, 10 metal buckets, 6 watering cans, 10 basins, 1 lifting jack, 20 brooms with handles, 10 long-handled scrubbing brushes. On the roof are four metal wheelbarrows. (L.Dv.783/6)

Trailer (long wooden type) for transporting 6 loading ramps for the pioneers' l.Z. (light Z-Bridge) bridge equipment. Two of these trailers belonged to a bridge construction set. Each loading ramp weighed 574.2 kg. Loaded weight of the trailer was 3,445 kg. (H.DV.220/3F)

Right: Amphibious trailer, built by the Kässbohrer Firm, for the Land-Water Tractor. (Spielberger)

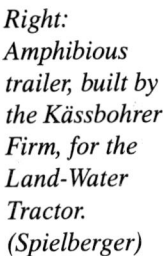

Frame-saw mounted on a trailer. Used by combat and railway engineers. Allowable loaded weight was 5,300 kg. (D 600)

Open trailer with a payload of 11,000 kg. This type of trailer was used mainly by motor transport regiments or battalions. (D 600)

Heavy amphibious trailer for the Land-Water Tractor with a payload of 20 tons. The trailer, built by Kässbohrer, could accept vehicles as large as an 18-ton prime mover. (W. Spielberger)

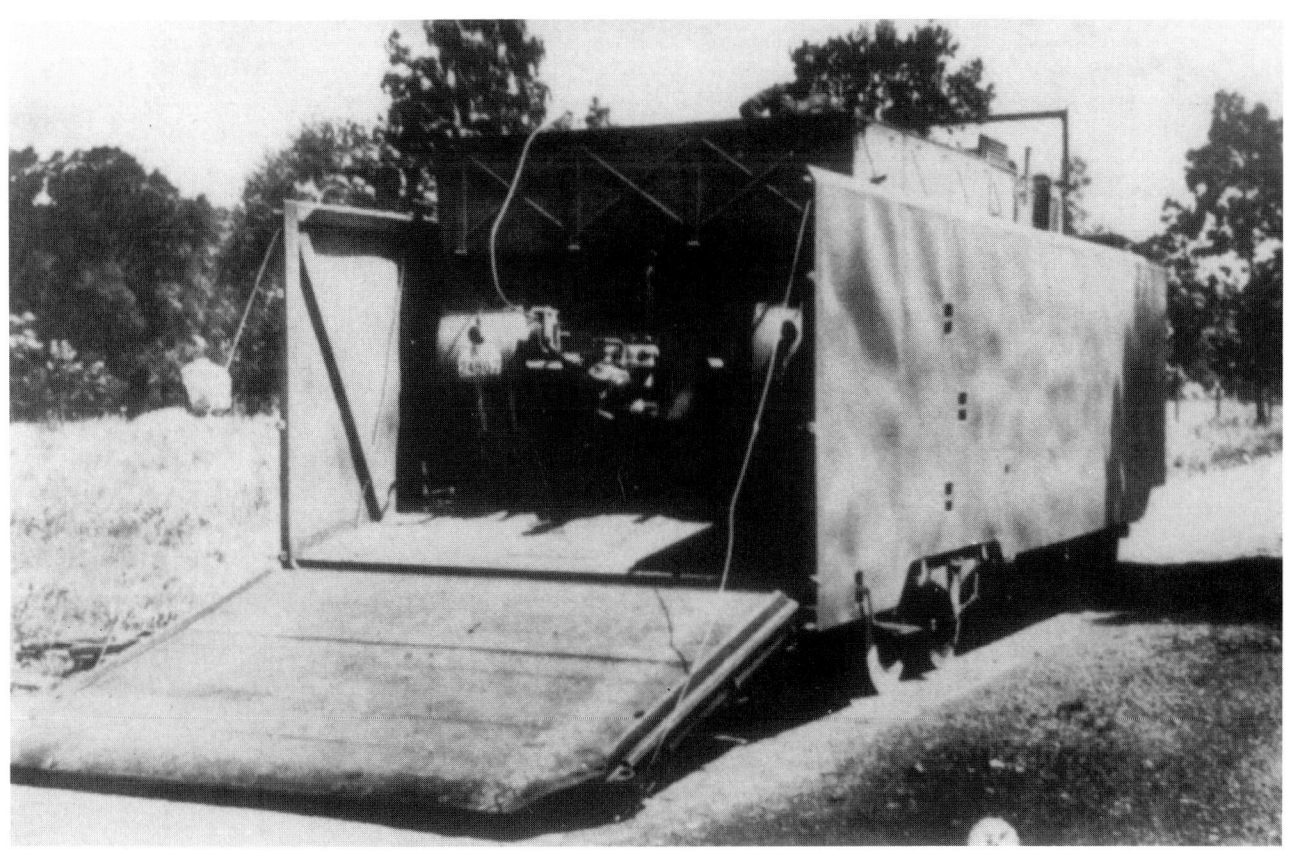

Left:
Mobile trailer-mounted version of the Strabo Crane with a lifting capacity of 16 tons. It was used by tank maintenance companies for removing tank turrets. Two of these cranes were also included in the technical batteries of long-range rocket units: one at the railway track for transferring the rockets from the railway car to the Vidal Trailer, and another for transferring the rockets from the Vidal Trailer to the Meiller Trailer at the battery launch site.

Below:
The Strabo Crane in travelling position.

Trailer with 30-ton crane by the Rheinmetall Firm for assembly of the "Karl" 600mm howitzer, which was transported by road in four loads. The photo shows the crane loaded disassembled for transport. (Rheinmetall)

The assembled 30-ton crane with the crane trailer on the hook. (Rheinmetall)

Culemeyer (four-axle) trailer for heavy loads, seen here carrying the upper carriage of the "Karl" 600mm howitzer. (Rheinmetall)

Culemeyer (six-axle) trailer for heavy loads with a payload of 60 tons. Here it is loaded with an Munitions-Panzer IV for serving the "Karl" howitzer. (Rheinmetall)

Above:
Six-axle trailer by the Gotha Rail Car Factory with a payload of 60 tons, seen here carrying a Jagdtiger (Sd.Kfz.186)

Right:
Twenty-four-wheel trailer for very heavy loads to 150 tons. (Spielberger)

Meiller Trailer for transporting the A 4 (V 2) long-range rocket to the firing position and raising it upright on the launch pad. Position Number 102 of the long-range rocket unit. Trailer length 14 meters. Weight of the rocket 4,500 kg.

The Spielberger German Armor & Military Vehicles Series

Size: 8 1/2" x 11"   288 pages   hard cover
over 460 photographs
ISBN: 0-88740-397-2 $39.95

Size: 8 1/2" x 11"   256 pages   hard cover
over 240 photographs
ISBN: 0-88740-398-0 $39.95

Size: 8 1/2" x 11"   168 pages   hard cover
over 200 photographs
ISBN: 0-88740-448-0 $29.95

Size: 8 1/2" x 11"   168 pages   hard cover
over 200 photographs
ISBN: 0-88740-515-0 $29.95